Feeding the Furnaces

Feeding the Furnaces: A History of Marquette's Iron Ore Dock No. 6

Russell M. Magnaghi

Feeding the Furnaces: A History of Marquette's Ore Dock No. 6
ISBN 978-1-257-65866-4

Northern Michigan University, 1401 Presque Isle Ave.,
Marquette, Michigan 49855
Email orders to rmagnagh@nmu.edu

TABLE OF CONTENTS

PREFACE

This book represents an attempt to bring into one account the story of the Lower Harbor ore dock, officially known as Marquette Ore Dock No. 6. This dock culminates the history of ore dock development within the Lake Superior Basin. The ore dock was developed in this region as a means to quickly unload iron ore and send the waiting ore boat on its way. The issue of cost to the shippers was paramount. Ore docks were found along the Lake Superior shoreline from Marquette to Ashland, Wisconsin and on to the largest collection of docks in the Duluth, Minnesota area. At one time a gravity feed ore dock was also found in Escanaba, Michigan. In Marquette there remain two ore docks – the Lower Harbor dock which dates from the early 1930s and the Upper Harbor dock which dates from 1912 and continues in use.

As will be seen, Marquette Ore Dock No. 6 has had a long history consisting of a number of ore docks on the site. As the technology and demand grew, ore docks were replaced, going from wooden docks to the concrete docks that remain. Unfortunately prior to this writing the information about the ore dock was locked in libraries and archives or within the pages of the Marquette *Mining Journal*. These materials were available to the serious researcher although time-consuming to reach. For the interested individual or visitor the information was all but unavailable. Many people who visited the Marquette Chamber of Commerce welcome center, overlooking the dock, would ask "what is that?" or "where can I get more information about the dock?"

The development of this monograph goes back to 1989 when serious discussions began between the city of Marquette and Wisconsin Central Ltd. Wisconsin Central had purchased the holdings of the Soo Line, the owners of the ore dock. A series of hearings were held in Marquette in 1989 to get the public's reaction to the removal of the trestle and the sale of the dock to the city. In the process I gave my views and left the hearing. A few months later I received a request from the Interstate Commerce Commission (ICC) to undertake the creation of a bibliography focusing on the history of the ore dock. I spent the summer gathering material from the Peter White Public Library and the Marquette Regional History Center's John Longyear Research Library. The folks at Wisconsin Central Ltd. were also very helpful which was critical to the project. Several months later I submitted my bibliographical report. At the time I thought that was the end of the study. It was not. The ICC wanted an architectural history of the ore dock which would chronicle the entire structure: Lower Harbor site, approach, dock, chutes and trestle. I worked on the project for many months following approved Federal guidelines which were linked to the official Historic American Engineering Record. Part of the guidelines stated that all materials connected with this project had to be copyright free and readily available to the American public. The architectural history includes not only the narrative but diagrams and photographs of the dock and surrounding area. During the research process the staff at Wisconsin Central Ltd. provided me with numerous priceless documents and photographs that have been deposited at the Upper Peninsula and University Archives on the campus of Northern Michigan University in Marquette. These are available to the public. After the completed report was accepted by the ICC it was deposited at the Library of Congress as Historic American Engineering Record (HAER MI-45A)

This work is available to the public through the Library of Congress. In recent years it is also available electronically. The Center for Upper Peninsula Studies decided to publish this work in hard-copy for the general public who may not be attracted to the electronic version or the many visitors to Marquette seeking a souvenir of their visit and the dock.

Research and publication of this work has been aided by numerous individuals. The staffs of Wisconsin Central Ltd, Peter White Public Library, and Marquette Regional History Center provided critical assistance with the research. Jack Deo, an independent photo technician and Dennis Staffne of Northern

Michigan University's Art and Design, Department Professor of photography provided invaluable service with the photographs. NMU student and alum Aaron Reider aided in preparing the early version of the manuscript. The final version was prepared by Toni Clisch. To all of these individuals we can all be thankful.

CHAPTER 1: EARLY HISTORY TO 1931

Development of Iron Mining

The former Duluth, South Shore & Atlantic (DSS&A) Ore Dock No. 6 is the physical legacy of nearly 140 years of history. Marquette was established in 1849 as a shipping point for iron ore which was extracted from the mines at Negaunee and Ishpeming some dozen miles inland. The dock is located in Marquette, Michigan's Lower Harbor. The structure juts into the harbor off of South Lakeshore Boulevard in the block between Main and Spring Streets. The approach to the dock, which was part of the overall complex, commenced at Fifth Street, some five blocks, or half-a mile, to the west.

The industrial history of the central Upper Peninsula of Michigan begins on September 19, 1844, when William Burt, deputy of the linear survey of the region, discovered iron ore in the present city of Negaunee. This and other ore bodies were located some dozen miles from the shore of Lake Superior.

As a result of this discovery of iron ore, the Marquette Range was developed within close proximity to transportation on Lake Superior. In 1845, a group of Jackson, Michigan speculators, headed by Philo M. Everett, explored the area and opened the Jackson Mine at Negaunee. Within the year, the first iron was mined from an open pit. A small iron forge was established at Carp River, a few miles to the east of the mine, and early in 1846, iron blooms were made from the Jackson ore. Then in 1849, the Cleveland Mine was developed near Ishpeming. In 1850, about five tons of ore were shipped from there to New Castle, Pennsylvania. News of the high quality of the ore spread among iron men in Pennsylvania and Ohio. Approximately seventy tons of ore were shipped from the Jackson mine to Sharon, Pennsylvania in 1852. It was the first Lake Superior ore to be made into pig iron. These experiments emphasized the value of this ore and it was realized that better transportation facilities to and from Lake Superior were necessary. With the opening of the St. Mary's River Canal at Sault Ste. Marie in 1855, which finally by-passed the twenty-seven foot drop between Lakes Superior and Huron, improvement in transportation of ore had begun.

Marquette as a Port City

The development of the city of Marquette as the major point of embarkation began because of the excellent harbor, which was improved over the years with the addition of a breakwater. In the summer of 1849, the future community and business leader Peter White, along with ten associates, arrived to develop a new community. While awaiting Amos Harlow and his crew and equipment, they visited the mines in the interior. By July 10, 1849, the various parties met at the future site of Marquette and began to clear the land. Anticipating the arrival of a supply ship, the laborers, under the direction of Sam Moody, constructed a dock, the first in the region. It was a crude affair of piled logs, stone, and sand located near the end of present-day Baraga Avenue (formerly Superior Street). Unfortunately, during the night of the third day of construction, the dock was completely destroyed by a lake storm. After that time, ships anchored a mile or two offshore and all goods and passengers were taken ashore by a lighter (flat barge). Animals that could swim were guided to shore. By the spring of 1850, there were a number of dwellings and shops concentrated at the foot of Baraga Avenue. The construction of a small dock allowed ships to land and ended the earlier inconvenience and inefficiency.

At first, the heavy iron ore was shipped over rough roads through a wilderness filled with mosquitoes and black flies. In 1856, a plank road was constructed from the mines to Marquette. It was soon converted into a tramway, and in 1857, it was supplanted by the Iron Mountain Railroad, the first in Upper Michigan. Previous to the construction of the railroad only 52,000 tons of ore were shipped and smelted at local forges. The entire output in 1857 was only 21,000 tons. The next year, production increased to 31,035 tons, and by 1860, it exceeded 100,000 tons.

Evolution of the Ore Dock to 1868

Over the years, the concept of the ore dock and ore boats evolved and was technologically refined as the demand for ore increased. When the first 1,447 tons of iron ore were shipped from Marquette, there was no loading dock. After cargo had been stored in the hold of small schooners and steamers, ore placed in a barrel was chiefly loaded on the decks.

The first ore dock ever constructed was built in Marquette's Lower Harbor in 1855 for the Jackson Iron Company by Jabez Smith of Sharon, Pennsylvania. It was located along the north side of the harbor where the Ellwood Mattson Park is located today. A wooden trestle extended from the end of Washington Street to the end of the dock. It gradually declined in height to about eight feet above the dock where the ore was unloaded. At this time, the ore was brought from the interior mines in mule drawn wooden wagons. The ore was shoveled from the wagons to the dock and then loaded into wheelbarrows and put into the hold of the waiting ships. It took twenty to thirty men several days to load two to three hundred tons of cargo. At that time the largest ships had a 300 ton capacity.

In the same year, the Cleveland Iron Mining Company built a dock at the foot of Baraga Avenue. In contrast to the Jackson dock, the wagons proceeded onto the level dock where the ore was unloaded into wheelbarrows and loaded aboard the vessels.

The first two docks proved to be inefficient. It was impractical to leave railroad cars loaded and standing idle until the arrival of a ship. In 1857, the Lake Superior Iron Company constructed a combination ore and merchandise dock at the foot of Main Street. This dock was twenty-five feet in height and was the first to have storage pockets for the ore. There were twenty-seven pockets on the south side of the dock with a capacity of two-thousand tons. The first ship captains feared that ore falling from that height would damage or possibly sink a vessel. These objections were soon overcome. In 1858, the Cleveland Dock was reconstructed with twenty-nine pockets and a capacity of 2,300 tons. Storage capacity was increased by raising the pockets to thirty feet while the mouth of the pocket remained at the same height.

The last of the pre-1868 ore docks was constructed in 1864 by the Bay de Noquet and Marquette Railroad. It was a combination ore and merchandise dock located on the site of Marquette Ore Dock No. 6 between Spring and Main Streets. It extended 600 feet into the harbor, was thirty-five feet in height, and had a capacity of approximately 4,000 tons.

Dock Construction to 1931

In June 1868, disaster struck Marquette. A fire broke out in the center of town and quickly engulfed most of the buildings and destroyed all of the ore docks except the Cleveland Dock. During the rest of the season, all of the mining companies used the Cleveland Dock twenty-four hours a day. Due to the great demand, ships had to anchor offshore for one to three weeks.

The Bay de Noquet and Marquette Railroad constructed a new dock in 1869 on the site of its old dock, of which 200 feet were spared in the fire. The new dock was larger than any of the older docks and showed technological improvement. It was 1,300 feet in length, thirty-eight feet high, over forty-six feet wide, and each of its 120 individual pockets held fifty-five tons, for a total capacity of 6,600 tons of ore. This dock was in operation until 1894.

Over the years, other ore docks were constructed, extended, or improved in Marquette's Lower Harbor. In 1905, the Duluth, South Shore & Atlantic Railroad (DSS&A) began constructing what became known as Dock No. 5. It was constructed on the site of the 1864 and 1869 docks. The wooden dock was 1,236 feet in length, seventy-one feet high, fifty-three feet and three inches wide, and its 200 pockets had a storage capacity of 40,000 tons of ore. The first boat was loaded in August 1906, and the last one left in November 1931.

Historical Development of the Lower Harbor Area

The Lower Harbor area of the city of Marquette extends from Baraga Avenue on the south to the bend in North Lakeshore Blvd. at the intersection of Bluff Street on the north. Originally, the lakeshore was approximately a city block or more to the west of the present shoreline. Over the years, this area of the city had been given over to commercial development related to the shipping of iron ore and receiving goods and passengers from lake steamers.

The city of Marquette was first settled at the foot of present day Baraga Avenue in July 1849. In the years that followed, given the importance of shipping iron ore and the development of docks, most of the community's attention was directed to the lakefront area. Over the years, a number of commercial and residential structures were erected in this area.

In the early summer of 1868, there were a few buildings along Lakeshore Blvd. On the corner of Baraga (then called Superior) Avenue and Lakeshore Blvd, the Burt brothers started the construction of a frame boarding house for Martin Vierling. While August Koch did own a dwelling in this area, most of the structures were of a commercial nature. C. Clune owned a building that was occupied by James Green, who lived above the saloon he operated there, one of two such establishments in the immediate vicinity. There were a number of warehouses in the area owned by Murray and Robbins and the Marquette & Ontonagon and Lake Superior & Ishpeming Railroads. These railroads and mining corporations such as the Jackson Iron Company had docks extending into Lake Superior. There were two fish houses owned by Jesse Goodwin and an ice house owned by Louis Reldinger. The Burt brothers had a lime kiln in the area and Thomas J. Pajot operated three pleasure boats from a dock. When the disastrous fire of June 11, 1868 struck, all of these properties were destroyed, amounting to over $125,000 in losses.

The commercial influence in the area continued through the early 1870s. A stairway connected upper Bluff Street and North Lakeshore Blvd. There were probably eight residents at this location. Only Charles S. Brown, a wagon maker, might have used the site for his business. Three clerks and a wagon maker, all named Brown, lived here along with two boiler makers, a bookkeeper and a molder. Elmer Anderson, a tinner, was the only resident in the intervening area, at Spring and Lake Streets. There was a cluster of commercial enterprises near the intersection of Lakeshore and Baraga. William Brimacombe and J. Cundy had their construction headquarters there, next to a saloon operated by Edward Carey. F.B.

Spear & Company, forwarding, commission, and steamboat agents also had their offices there. A lone bookkeeper, A.B. Taylor, was the only resident in the area other than the folks at the Bluff Street site. Trestle approaches to the ore docks crossed South Lakeshore Blvd. and there were ore and merchandise docks extending into the lake. These docks were, from north to south: Jackson Dock, off Washington Street; followed by the railroad merchandise dock; railroad ore dock; and the Cleveland Company's merchandise and ore dock, at the foot of Baraga Avenue.

Evidence of the filling process could be seen as early as 1871. The largest amount of fill is found along the shoreline in the vicinity of Washington Street. With the construction of the Jackson Dock, a lagoon was created between the dock and the north shoreline, a haven for small boats and a few fish houses.

The next view of the area is found on an 1881 lithograph of Marquette. By that time, the eastern portion of the lagoon had been filled and was the site of the Grace Iron Furnace. The cluster of four fish houses at the west end of the lagoon would be the nucleus of future structures. The dwellings at Bluff Street had expanded along the base of the hill to the north. The trestles leading to the MH&O and Merchandise Docks and the Christiana and City Hotels, operated by C.J. Hansen and P.C. Miller, respectively, were located between Main and Baraga. The "Custom House" and the property of F.B. Spears & Sons were both located at the foot of Baraga Avenue. There was a steep drop from Lakeshore Blvd to the shore.

The on-going development and change along both sides of Lakeshore Blvd can be reconstructed by utilizing a series of Sanborn insurance maps for 1884, 1888, 1892, 1897, 1904, 1917, 1928, and 1934-1946.

By 1884, at the bottom of the Bluff Street stairs, there were two dwellings and an ice house. Beyond that, towards Washington Street, the Iron Bay Manufacturing Company's foundry had been established. The block between Washington and Main was empty except for two small structures. The southwest corner of Main and Lakeshore Blvd was occupied by the sandstone office building of the Marquette, Houghton, & Ontonagon Railroad, which was constructed in 1872. On the same block were a saloon and a combination saloon/boarding house. The structures, from north to south, between Spring Street and Baraga Avenue included a flour and feed store, a machine shop, a saloon, a saloon/boarding house, a horse shed, and another saloon/boarding house.

On the east, or lake side, of the street was the F.B. Spears & Sons wood, fuel, building supplies, and feed operation. The structures on the property consisted of a variety of small storage sheds and offices built on fill land, leased from the railroad, extending approximately a city block into the lake. There were two adjacent lime kilns and a wood pile between Main and Washington Streets.

By 1888, the west side of Lakeshore Blvd, on the corner of Main, was dominated by The Casino, a large two story structure with a livery stable on the first floor and a large indoor recreation facility upstairs. It was used as a concert hall and a venue for indoor baseball games, ice skating, theater, wrestling matches, and many other activities. This structure faced the lake and was directly to the rear of the present day Vierling Restaurant. Unfortunately, this facility gained an unsavory reputation, and the February 15, 1890 edition of the Marquette *Mining Journal* reported that it was a "disgrace to Marquette to put it mildly." The Casino was purchased by the Flanagan Brothers in 1915, and was used for storage and as a garage until it burned to the ground on December 31, 1931, in a spectacular fire which saw nearly a dozen cars and a truck explode. Except for this structure and the shore line of Baraga, which was being filled, the area remained the same.

During the 1890s, there were few changes in the district. The Iron Bay Manufacturing Company was now the Lake Superior Iron Works. The James Pickands & Company Coal Dock had been established on the lakefront at the end of Spring Street. The Duluth, South Shore, & Atlantic was utilizing the old Customs House for storage. Many of the saloons and boarding houses between Baraga and Spring were vacant, probably due to the recent depression which hit the nation at that time.

By 1904, Lake Superior Iron Works was called Lake Shore Engine Works. There was a slight expansion of the fish houses and net drying sheds at the foot of Washington Street. The saloons and boarding houses between Baraga and Spring continued to be vacant.

The following Lake Street businesses appear in the 1910 city directory:

Location	Business
117 N. Lakeshore Blvd	*Gannon Grocery Company*
119-123 N. Lakeshore Blvd	*Pioneer Motor Company*
Intersection of Washington Street (lake side)	*Andrew Anderson (fish wholesaler)*
Foot of Washington Street (lake side)	*John Parker (fish wholesaler)*
Foot of East Main Street (lake side)	*Peter Anderson (fish wholesaler)*
Northwest corner of Lakeshore and Main	*Fay & Bricker Livery*
Foot of East Baraga Avenue	*F.B. Spears & Sons (building materials and supplies)*
Foot of East Baraga Avenue	*Marquette Stone Company*

The vacancies continued in 1911, although a number of fish houses were erected. Lake Shore Engine Works was taken over by Gannon Wholesale Grocers and Lake Superior & Ishpeming Railroad opened a passenger station on the northwest corner of Washington Street and Lakeshore Blvd. Except for the addition of a few more fish houses, the area remained relatively unchanged by 1917.

In 1924, the north end of the Lakeshore Blvd saw a great change take place. F.B. Spear & Sons, who had been operating out of facilities at the foot of Baraga Avenue, purchased the lagoon and property owned by the Grace Furnace Company. They filled the area and developed a large coal landing facility which was operated by the Marquette Dock Company, a joint venture of F.B. Spears & Sons and Pickands. The area was dominated by a mammoth steel unloading crane called the “coal bridge.” Naturally, this development precipitated the demise of many of the fish houses located in and around the lagoon, though a few remained to the south of the coal dock. Also as a result of this development, the old Pickands coal dock was slated for removal sometime after 1928. However, in July 1930, it was partially destroyed by fire.

The Casino building was still in use as a fifty capacity automobile garage and bus station. The 1872 sandstone structure on the corner of Lakeshore Blvd and Main Street was used as a dock office. Directly south of this was the Lake Shore Iron Works. In the block between Spring and Baraga, most of the former vacant saloons and boarding houses had been turned into furniture and rug storage warehouses for the furniture store on Front Street. Other structures had been given over to the storage of automobile parts and painting supplies.

The additions to the 1928 map, made in 1934 and 1946, show some minor changes. A few fish houses remained near the foot of Washington Street. A clubhouse was added, along with two coal brickette manufacturing structures. The 1946 Sanborn map shows a cement block factory between Main and Spring Streets, next to the F.B. Spears & Sons feed mill and fuel lot. Near the lake was a private garage with room for thirteen trucks.

There was very little change along Marquette's lakefront between 1946 and 1976. Because of the July 1, 1976 opening of a new coal unloading facility at the Upper Peninsula Power Company, there was no longer a need for the Marquette Dock Company's facilities at the foot of Washinghton Street. The coal era at Lower Harbor ended in September of 1976, and F.B. Spears & Sons was now the sole owner of the property. Eventually, the Spears property was sold to the city of Marquette, and, during the 1980s, the Ellwood Mattson Park was developed on the former site of the coal dock. The city of Marquette continued work to further develop this area into a recreational site.

Between 1990 and 2012 the Lakeshore Blvd. area was transformed from construction-related businesses – building, painting, glass, plumbing, iron works – to service businesses – restaurants, condos and professional offices. At last Marquette reached a point in its existence that it turned toward Lake Superior and embraced it, much as Chicago did many years earlier.

CHAPTER 2: GENERAL HISTORY OF ORE DOCK NO. 6

Early Studies and Plans for a New Ore Dock

The dock known as Ore Dock No. 6 juts into Marquette's Lower Harbor off Lakeshore Blvd between Main and Spring Streets. It is a direct descendant of the many ore docks which have stood in Marquette's Lower Harbor. DSS&A officials estimated that the life of Ore Dock No. 5, constructed in 1905-06, was only twenty-five years. As a result, in 1926, the company began to develop plans for a new dock. A steel and concrete dock was deemed more practical than one made of wood, as evidenced by the 1896 dock built at Presque Isle on the north side of town. From 1926 to 1930, data was assembled, preliminary surveys made, and diamond drill tests conducted of the harbor bottom.

In 1930 the Chief Engineer of DSS&A reported that the timber ore dock could not be maintained in a safe operating condition beyond the 1931 shipping season and a new dock would have to be constructed as planned. The old dock was proving very expensive to maintain and operate. The average repairs costs between 1916 and 1930 amounted to 14,000 dollars annually. On account of the fire hazard, insurance costs were high, and watchmen had to be employed around the clock. Furthermore, from an operational standpoint the dock was obsolete. Due to its insufficient height from the water, the larger boats could not be loaded to their maximum capacity, considerable ore was spilled into the slips, and serious delays were encountered by all of the boats. Since quick dispatch was imperative during the shipping season, the company was subjected to numerous complaints.

In early March 1929, there was talk that construction would begin immediately, but final plans were not completed until the fall of 1930. Furthermore, there were technical problems to be dealt with by the railroad. At the end of the year the railroad received permission from the Marquette City Commission to proceed with construction.

Financing the Dock

At this time, the DSS&A was without funds to build a new dock. Without a dock it would lose its iron ore business, which represented 25% to 40% of its total tonnage and 11% to 20% of its earnings. This would have a disastrous affect on the company's earning capacity and on its bond-holders. The financial problems were fully explained to officials of the Canadian Pacific Railway Company. In order to protect the future earnings of the company, Canadian Pacific advanced South Shore $350,000 toward the cost of the new dock and made certain additional guaranties. A corporation known as the South Shore Dock Company, with a capital of $10,000 (subsequently reduced to $1,000), was organized by the South Shore Railway Company. The articles of association were filed at the Marquette County Court House on March 11, 1931.

The proposed site for the new dock was on a piece of property on which the Marquette, Houghton & Ontonagon mortgage, dated April 1, 1885, was a first lien and was also subject to the liens of the DSS&A mortgages of April 15, 1887 and July 17, 1890. This property was deeded to the South Shore Dock Company after releases had been obtained from the Marquette, Houghton & Ontonagon and South Shore Railway Company mortgages, giving the Dock Company unencumbered title to the site. It constructed the dock at a cost of approximately $1,350,000 and leased it to the Marquette, Houghton & Ontonagon Railroad Company for a period of 14 and one half years at a rental of $4,166.67 per month up to and including the end of November 1931, and $8,350 per month from December 1, 1931 to November 30, 1945, in order to provide for interest charges and serial retirement of bonds. This lease was later assigned to the South Shore Railway Company.

To provide funds for this dock in excess of the money advanced by the Canadian Pacific, the South Shore Dock Company executed a first mortgage and issued $1,000,000 worth of bonds and pledged the dock and the lease as security. The payment of the lease rentals was guaranteed by the Canadian Pacific Railway.

The Awarding of Contracts

The construction process began with the awarding of contracts. The first one was awarded in March 1931, when the Lake Shore Engine Works of Marquette was contracted to construct 150 hoists for raising and lowering the dock chutes. The second contract was let out on April 1 of that year to the Merritt, Chapman & Whitney Corporation of Duluth. This company was the successor to Whitney Bros., which specialized in the building of docks, bridges, and river and harbor improvements.

The fabricated steel for the dock, including the large steel ore chutes, would be furnished by McClintick & Marshall Corporation of Chicago. Jernstad Electric of Ishpeming would install the electrical work and the Woden & Allen Company of Chicago was given the contract for furnishing all of the project's reinforced steel.

Labor Force

The project's labor force was primarily from the Marquette area. Since the country was in the heart of the Great Depression, the Marquette Chamber of Commerce requested the DSS&A officials to pressure Merritt, Chapman & Whitney to hire Marquette laborers. By mid-May, rumors began to circulate that out-of-town workmen had been employed on the site. A quick investigation showed that Merritt, Chapman & Whitney had brought in their own engineers and men familiar with pile driving. These laborers were brought in because pile driving was dangerous for unskilled laborers and it would have taken three months to train a Marquette work force. At the time, 75% of the on-site workers were from Marquette, and it was pointed out that more laborers would be needed to construct the land approach. By July 7, the dock construction crew reached its maximum size although a few more men might be necessary in the fall if unfavorable weather should slow up the operations, which were already running a little behind schedule.

There were approximately 325 men working in two shifts. Given the nature of concrete work, these crews were employed twenty-four hours a day while the rest worked two ten hour shifts. The percentage of Marquette workers remained the same. For a month at the height of construction, there were 340 men working on the site, but that figure soon returned to approximately 250-275 men. Toward the end of the construction season in late October, there were 290 on the payroll. As the dock neared completion in early November, the labor demand was far less, and by February 1932, as completion of the dock approached, the work force was down to 155 men.

Injuries

Serious injuries on the work site were infrequent. On September 30, however, Floyd Balwanski fell twenty feet from the dock to the bottom of a pocket. He was taken to St. Luke's Hospital in Marquette with two fractured ribs, a fractured wrist, torn ligaments, and facial lacerations. It took him several months of recuperating before he returned to work. In mid-December, the first fatal accident was reported: Edward Magnuson of Twin Harbors, Minnesota fell from the dock into the water and struck a piece of floating timber. He died several days later from internal injuries.

The fact that dock construction work provided jobs for several hundred Marquette residents did not go unnoticed. In late January 1932, they contributed a percentage of their wages, amounting to $308, to the Family Welfare Agency of Marquette.

Work on the dock was blessed with excellent weather. There were a number of hot spells which drove temperatures into triple digits, but they soon passed and Marquette's cool summer weather prevailed. Between April and September, 1931, only half a day had been lost due to the weather. This mild weather continued through December and allowed work to progress ahead of schedule.

Demolition of the Old Dock and Construction

The shipping season closed on November 16, with the loading and departure of the *George R. Fink*, bound for Buffalo, New York. Prior to the actual razing of the timber dock, the chutes and hoists were removed and taken to the DSS&A west yards where they were stored for future disposition. Beginning December 1, between sixty and seventy men were employed razing the old dock. Work progressed rapidly. The electrical work was dismantled and attention was directed toward dismantling the steel trestle over Front Street. The DSS&A salvaged and sold the larger timbers, while the scrap wood and small timber was shipped to the Schneider Sawmill in north Marquette. The work of dismantling the old dock was all but completed in early February 1932, and by the end of the month, the refuse material and old timbers were removed from the site.

At the site of the new dock some last winterization was taking place. The huge traveling crane which straddled the dock and was used as a mount for booms was dismantled and stored. One tug and the barges *Four Spot* and *The Limit* were wintered in Marquette. DSS&A cars were loaded with other pieces of equipment and shipped to Duluth.

In early February 1932, Merritt, Chapman & Whitney reported that the construction project was two months ahead of schedule, making the new projected completion date March 1. Electrical equipment and machinery had to be installed, along with general finishing work such as cleaning and painting.

Cost of Construction

The dock was fully completed and ready for operation on May 15, 1932. The total cost to the companies involved was as follows:

Paid Constructors	$558,716.72
Materials Purchased	$501,597.02
Freight charges on materials	$108,617.56
Rental of equipment	$3.00
Land and improvements	$32,863.48
Discount on bonds	$30,000.00
Michigan mortgage tax	$5,000.00
Engineering and other expenses	$86,616.82
Total	**$1,320,414.60**

The South Shore Dock Company expended the following monies:

From its own funds.................. $350,000.00
From funds received from trustees
on certificates nos. 1 to 9,
inclusive.................................... $593,184.48

The Duluth, South Shore and Atlantic Railway Company expended:

From funds received from trustees on
certificates nos. 10 to 20,
inclusive.................................... $374,635.12
From its own funds subject to
reimbursement by trustees...... $2,595.00

First Shipment

Although the dock was completed, the Depression economy slowed its use. Most of the mines on the Range had been closed since November 1931, because of the lack of steel orders. The Ford Motor Company's Blueberry Mine in Ishpeming was open but only operating at half capacity. It had accumulated a stockpile of 10,000 tons of iron ore which could be shipped from the new dock. DSS&A officials anxiously awaited the first shipment.

The new dock was put into service on June 3, 1932, when thirty cars arrived from the Blueberry Mine and offloaded the ore into the dock. At 1:20 p.m., on 6 June, 10,103 tons of ore were loaded into the Detroit-bound *Henry Ford II.* On June 19, that same vessel returned and loaded 3,000 tons of Imperial Mine ore and 7,000 tons of Blueberry Mine ore. The actual loading time was 2 hours and 58 minutes. The loss of time was due to sticky ore from the Imperial Mine and a shortage of help.

Shipments, 1932-1971

Over the next thirty-nine years, the following tonnage was shipped from Ore Dock No. 6*:

Year	Tonnage	Year	Tonnage
1932	*122,314*	1952	*398,110*
1933	*442,496*	1953	*471,108*
1934	*636,353*	1954	*309,779*
1935	*617,826*	1955	*474,309*
1936	*941,473*	1956	*492,023*
1937	*867,367*	1957	*361,362*
1938	*178,539*	1958	*491,371*
1939	*639,622*	1959	*628,577*
1940	*642,837*	1960	*600,713*
1941	*860,674*	1961	*499,792*
1942	*684,603*	1962	*597,648*
1943	*601,735*	1963	*681,079*
1944	*308,306*	1964	*844,697*
1945	*516,436*	1965	*1,068,355*
1946	*340,299*	1966	*1,158,617*
1947	*524,055*	1967	*875,307*
1948	*437,839*	1968	*1,018,068*
1949	*462,729*	1969	*1,108,316*
1950	*619,469*	1970	*590,972*
1951	*578,876*	1971	*258,039*

**The greatest tonnage year for either Ore Dock No. 5 or No. 6 was in 1911, when 1,383,206 tons of iron ore were shipped.*

Statistics: Materials and Dimensions

Upon the dock's completion, its dimensions were not exceeded by any other dock in the Lake Superior region. It was composed of the following materials:

Dock:

Structural steel................. 1,740 tons
Concrete........................... 28,650 cubic yards
Reinforcing steel................ 1,370 tons
CI snubbing posts............. 11.5 tons
Hardware and iron........... 30 tons
Piling timbers..................... 7,600 foot board measure

Approach:

Structural steel.................. 945.5 tons
Concrete............................ 1,360 cubic yards
Reinforcing steel................. 9.35 tons
Hardware and iron............ 34 tons
Pilings............................... 19,580 foot board measure
Timber............................. 840,000 foot board measure

The length of the facility, including both the approach and the dock, was 3,546 feet. The dock itself measured 969 feet from the beginning of concrete construction to the fender at the east end.

During its first year in service, the dock handled a mere 122,314 tons. Planned in the prosperous 1920s, it had potential for increased use in the future. Throughout its history, Ore Dock No. 6 was maintained and improved; however, there were no major renovations which completely altered the nature and utilization of the structure.

The Dock during World War II

During World War II, Ore Dock No. 6 operated efficiently although not at full capacity. Even in Marquette there was concern for espionage, and on July 8, 1943, Walter Measure from the Continuous Security Branch of the Sixth Army inspected the facility. In a report issued on July 20, it was recommended that the railroad provide riot guns or sawed-off shotguns for its guards; properly train the guards in the use of these firearms; and increase the number of fire extinguishers throughout the timber deck area. The next year, two wooden semaphores were placed at the end of the dock to signal approaching boats which side was available for loading. The dock entry lights were useful at night but, because of the glare, captains could not see them during the day.

Developments 1947-1971

Major improvements were made at the end of the 1947 season. The wooden fenders on the dock were rebuilt and pile drivers re-drove the cluster piles. By mid-October, the pilings for the protective fenders at the outer end of the ore dock had been re-driven, though they had not been spaced nor the timber blocks installed. The cluster piles near Ripley's Rock to the south were re-driven and tied with cable. On the south side of the dock, all of the pilings in the wood fender were re-driven but not cut off. The schedule called for work to be completed by the end of the month.

Due to the harsh weather conditions, repairs and improvements were constantly made on the dock. In early 1953, it was observed that the overhead wiring on the upper deck was in need of replacement. This work was completed by 1957. In 1961, poor lighting at the end of the dock necessitated the installation of a flood light and two other lights twelve feet above the fender. The electric hoist motors received gradual maintenance and repair at the rate of two motors per year between 1956 and the early 1960s.

The last major repair program dates back to 1954, however, during the early 1960s, there were a number of heavy repairs made on the dock. During the winters of 1965-66 and 1966-67, general dock work was carried out along with the construction of approach posts, and bridge piling. Costly steel work on the chute liners and ore pocket doors was also completed, along with repairs to the wooden decking and walkways. Finally, the untreated dock timbers were replaced with rot resistant treated timbers.

Besides the maintenance to the structure there were concerns for the depth of the slips for ships. Silt build-up necessitated periodic and detailed soundings of the north and south slips. Although the depth was usually adequate, offshore winds lowered the water level to a dangerous minimum and thus dredging had to be done. In 1954, nearly 22,300 cubic yards of silt were removed from both sides of the dock. Again in 1965, 21,500 cubic yards were removed from the north side only. Ripley's Rock along the south side limited ships to a depth of twenty-five feet.

Ownership of the Dock

Over the years, Ore Dock No. 6 was owned by a number of railroads. On March 11, 1931, the South Shore Dock Company was incorporated to manage the facility for the DSS&A Railroad. This company was finally dissolved on September 13, 1943. The DSS&A was bought by the Soo Line in 1961; new owners continued to operate the dock the same as it was in the past. Finally, Wisconsin Central Ltd. purchased the Ore Dock and other Marquette Soo Line properties in October 1987.

Origin of the Iron Shipments

The life of the ore dock was based on ore production of the once numerous small, independent mines on the Marquette Range. Cleveland Cliffs Iron Company (CCI), the major producer on the Range, had its own ore dock at Presque Isle in north Marquette. By 1970, Ore Dock No. 6 was receiving most of its ore from the Tracy Mine, owned by the Jones & Laughlin Steel Corp., in Negaunee. This underground mine, which shipped its first ore on September 10, 1955, supplied iron ore to company steel mills in Cleveland, Pittsburgh, and elsewhere. In 1962, the mine reached its peak of production, employing over 350 men. In early 1971, Robert Prittenen announced to a stunned and silent Negaunee City Council meeting, attended by miners, that the mine would be closed. He cited the fact that the ore was unsalable on the market due to the fact that it was between only 11- 13% iron, while pelletized ore was 63-66% iron. Construction of a pellet plant was not possible because the mine was only one-tenth the size of CCI's Mather Mine in Negaunee.

As a result of this development, the 1971 shipping season at the dock was short. The first ship was loaded on May 4, and only fifty more followed. The last ore car left the Tracy Mine on July 9, and on July 28, the *J. Hutchinson* was the last vessel to load from the dock. Throughout the season, only 258,039 tons of ore were shipped from the Lower Harbor dock. Between 1932 and 1971, nearly twenty-four million tons of ore was shipped from the Ore Dock No. 6, averaging 598,777.25 tons per year. In contrast, the season at the Lake Superior & Ishpeming Dock at Presque Isle, which handled CCI ore, ran from April 13 to December 8, 1971. 201 ships were loaded with 3,157,474 tons of ore. As a result, the Soo Line made the decision to terminate service at the Lower Harbor dock on December 31 of that year.

Post-1971 Attempts at Re-Activating the Dock

After the dock closed in 1971, there were a number of attempts to reopen it. With the development of ore pellets, whereby low grade iron ore was crushed, the waste removed, and a new enriched pellet created, the Marquette Range had new life. One of the major projects on the Range was the development of the Tilden Mine. In early 1974, officials with the Soo Line and Cleveland Cliffs Iron Company discussed the possibility of reopening Dock No 6. At the time, the Tilden Mine was expected to commence production on July 1, 1974, at the rate of four million tons per year. It was anticipated that this production would rise to around eight million tons in 1978. By 1982, the projected figure was nearly twelve million tons. It was hoped that within eight to ten years the mine would be producing somewhere around twenty million tons of pellets. The Lake Superior & Ishpeming Railroad Dock in north Marquette and the Escanaba facilities on Lake Michigan could not handle this tremendous increase in production, so Soo Line officials were asked to consider reopening the old dock. A complete inspection was conducted in July 1972, and the dock and its approach were found to be in fairly good condition. There was some wear on the concrete in the pockets which would require future maintenance. The major work required on the dock, however, would be the replacement of damaged and rotted planking on the deck proper, the straightening of chute angles, the installation of splash shields at the chutes, some welding on the chutes, and the replacement of some timber fenders. All of the electric motors, which were last operated the spring of 1973, appeared to be in good condition as well. Soundings along both sides of the dock were taken on December 28, 1973, and it was found that dredging was necessary in order to efficiently utilize the facility.

A cost repair estimate was made by the Soo Line. The repairs to the dock and its approaches would be $38,000, while dredging would cost an additional $65,000. $6,000 would have to be spent on the installation of splash shields on the pockets. Besides the regular maintenance, it was anticipated that if the dock shipped 1.5 million ton of ore per year it would have to be extensively rehabilitated in 2004. Unfortunately, nothing followed these reports.

In 1981, there was renewed interest in utilizing the dock and its approaches. A complete inspection of the dock showed that it would have to be rehabilitated if it were to be reopened. The report showed the deck proper to be in poor condition and that most of the ties would have to be replaced. The shakers and doors were beyond repair and would have to be replaced. Further, ninety-three front covers and eighty-one rear covers on the chutes were missing. Because the sanitary facilities drained directly into the lake, they would have to be connected to the city sewer system. The hoists needed repaired, along with the stairs and the ore scale, which was destroyed by fire. The approach needed many replacements and it was recommended that the rails and switches be replaced with heavier gauge rails to more efficiently handle heavier loads. The Soo Line estimated proposed expenses according to the following schedule:

Dock and approach	$625,000
Dock electrical equipment And motors	$19,000
Dredging (contract work)	$70,000

In the course of the correspondence, a review of the historical development of the structure was brought forth. Although the original cost of the structure was $1,297,900 in 1981 it would have cost $13,789,927 to replace the dock. Over the years the structure and its marine approaches had were improved according to the following schedule:

Improvements	**Years**	**Cost**
Electrical work	1933-44	$323
Fenders	1947	$19,322
Dredging	1954	$9,935
Dredging one slip	1965	$30,084
Approach Improvement	1958	$21,320
Approach Improvement	1959	$29,124

The status of the dock remained undecided. On March 8, 1985, Krech & Ojard Consulting Engineers, based in Duluth, Minnesota released a report, "Removal Estimate of the Soo Line Ore Dock in Marquette MI," which had been ordered by the Michigan Department of Transportation. The demolition was to: 1) remove the dock superstructure to elevation 610.35, roughly nine feet above Mean Low Water; 2) remove the dock foundation; and 3) remove the approach trestle to the dock. This had to be done because a land title search found that the submerged land on which the ore dock was constructed was owned by the State of Michigan. Michigan's Great Lakes Submerged Lands Act (1945) requires that all structures which were constructed in state waters have to be removed when the use of the facility is terminated. At the time, the cost estimate for demolition was:

Removal of the timber portion of the approach, the dock superstructure to elevation 610.35, and the outer timber trestle	$3,039,454
Removal of the dock foundation below elevatioin 610.35	$1,419,833
Removal of the steel portion of the dock approach together with the timber decking and concrete piers	$70,635
Total Net Cost	$4,529,922

The question of vandalism, trespass, liability, and fire has been raised and dealt with since the construction of the structure. During World War II there was concern with sabotage, and the dock was guarded as a precaution. The question of using the dock to unload petroleum products and gasoline was raised by the International Oil Company in May 1950. The company wanted to run a pipeline along the dock to its storage tanks in the vicinity. DSS&A officials, citing a high fire danger to an extremely important facility, declined the offer even though it meant the loss of tanker car traffic on the line.

State of Michigan and the Dock

In November 1986, the dispute over the dock between the state of Michigan and the Soo Line took a new twist. Attorney General Frank Kelley brought a lawsuit in Ingham County in an attempt to halt any sale of the dock unless the potential buyer was financially able to remove the structure. The suit not only involved the ore dock, but pilings which remained above water level throughout Lower Harbor. The state was primarily concerned with liability and clear title to the bottomlands under the dock either had to be transferred to the railroad or gained through a long-term lease.

However, on October 11, 1987, before a number of depositions could be taken the Soo Line sold the ore dock to Wisconsin Central Ltd. The lawsuit was temporarily suspended. In the meantime, Wisconsin Central began the process of selling excess property. The railroad entered into discussions with Marquette City Manager David Svanda. The city wanted to have the approach removed to enhance the downtown area. The Interstate Commerce Commission (ICC) stated, however, that the removal of the approach would have an "adverse" effect on the structure's historical value. The Michigan Bureau of History agreed with this action. The ICC wanted a report conducted which would study the impact of the sale or alternations of the ore dock and how this would affect the integrity of the structure.

Before any action could be taken to dismantle even part of the dock, the former Interstate Commerce Commission requested a detailed architectural and historical survey of the dock. Dr. Russell

Magnaghi, regional historian and member of the Northern Michigan University faculty, was hired to conduct the research and narrative of the dock. The Commission saw the dock as a historical structure to be preserved in written and photographic form. The final report was deposited in the Library of Congress as public record.

During the decade of the 1990s Wisconsin Central Ltd. Negotiated with a variety of state and federal regulatory agencies for the removal of the timber and iron trestles. The process began in 1990 when Wisconsin Central petitioned the Surface Transportation Board, then the Interstate Commerce Commission for abandonment of the track atop the trestle. Upper Peninsula Engineers and Architects were influential in obtaining the STB abandonment permit and an earlier permit from the Michigan Department of Environmental Quality. In the summer of 1999 the STB approved the track abandonment which opened the way for the removal of the trestle.

The city of Marquette was long eager to have the trestle removed as it was felt by many that it cut the downtown in half. In early 1990, the city proposed to remove the trestle and build a one-way street along its right-of-way. The idea was that this street would parallel Washington Street and the two streets would become one-way thoroughfares, thus easing traffic congestion in downtown Marquette. Nothing came of this early plan. At times plans were temporarily halted by groups and individuals who presented plans to redevelop the ore dock into condos and shops creating what some considered would be a major tourist attraction in downtown Marquette. Many of these plans were well intended but they lacked the necessary financial capital.

There was much debate, however, as to the historical value of the section of trestle over Front Street. By some, this section of track was seen as a symbolic "entrance" to the city, yet most agreed that it was little more than a rusting eyesore that would cost the city tens of thousands of dollars to maintain.

After many starts and stops in late December 1999 the Marquette City Commission voted 5 to one to remove the trestle, including the portion over Front Street. A public pathway would replace the iron trestle from Lakeshore Blvd. to the vicinity of Fourth Street. This final plan has been implemented much to the satisfaction of the city and its residents.

Upper Peninsula Engineers and Architects was the firm that dismantled the trestle. The first section of the iron trestle over Lakeshore Blvd. came down on January 11, 2000. Workers carefully unbolted and cut the section which weighed 28,000 pounds, from its location more than eighty feet above the street. A massive 300-ton capacity crane, owned and operated by Lunda Construction of Black Falls, Wisconsin, which towered over the trestle, slowly lowered sections to the ground onto flat bed trucks. The sections were then hauled to a Wisconsin Central storage facility in Wisconsin to be reused on future projects. The removal of the trestle continued. By March 2000 the wooden trestle was gone and the iron portions were coming down.

Remains of the trestle lay along the route for many months afterward and were slowly removed. Finally all that remained to be done was to remove the concrete supports in various locations. The concrete abutments on Fourth Street were removed in September of 2005 to make way for the new bike path. In January of 2006, the last standing remnant of the trestle, the lone concrete abutment on the west side of Front Street, was slated for removal, and it was demolished soon afterward. The removal of the trestle finished at last.

Proposed Reuses of the Ore Dock

The ore dock fascinates visitors, most of whom want to know what the structure is and how it was used. Other people see it as an eyesore, while local residents view it as a rich and historic part of the Marquette landscape, looming over and guarding the Lower Harbor.

Since the 1980s various ambitious and creative individuals have looked on the ore dock as the base for economic development and the tourist trade. The various proposals have ranged from a tourism-type attraction on top of the dock, to its use as a rail line, location for retail shops, a museum, and most recently a botanical-ecological center.

During the 1980s, the residents of Marquette reevaluated the use of the Lake Superior shoreline around the ore dock. The old Spear coal dock was purchased by the city of Marquette and gradually turned into an attractive and popular city park, home to major celebrations and events. In May 1986, the Marquette Area Chamber of Commerce Tourist Council Ore Dock Committee, chaired by Frank Stabile, formulated an idea of integrating the dock into the general development of the area as it would relate to tourism. One was to use the dock as a rail terminal for a tourist-focused train trip from the dock to Ishpeming and back. Another idea called for retail shops. This latter idea was further developed in the "Lower Harbor Redevelopment Plan" created by Gove Associates and issued in July 1986. This was a general plan for the whole Lower Harbor area. The plan called for a boardwalk at lake level with enclosed pedestrian bridge with small specialty retail shops. The shops would have been located on the top of the dock in a mall lined with potted trees and an iron museum at the lake end. In this plan, Front Street would have been connected with the top of the dock. The other possibility was to remove the structure, leaving a dock eight to ten feet above water level for pedestrian and vehicle traffic. As these plans were being developed Attorney General Frank Kelley brought a lawsuit in a downstate court to have all of the remnants of the six earlier docks removed from the site. Nothing came of this action except that there were a number of public hearings which brought out many members of the community to voice their opinions as to what should happen with the dock.

As these plans were being developed, they were being done without a lack of ownership of the ore dock by the city of Marquette, so planning was limited. Little could be done with the railway because the Soo Line was being sold. In October 1987, Wisconsin Central, Ltd. purchased the Soo Line Railroad Company's Upper Peninsula holdings. The new owner having no use of the ore dock and seeking monetary gain stated that it planned on removing the trestle and additions to the dock for safety reasons. Although the stairway to the top of the dock was technically secure from trespassers, its rusty barbed wire and gate was easily by-passed by youths who climbed to the top. Obviously the new owners were concerned with liability.

After nearly a decade of discussions the approaches to the ore dock were removed in 1999 through 2000. Although visitors and residents had their ideas and opinions about the dock, little was proposed. One visiting Italian businessman around 2011 thought a revolving restaurant on the top of the dock would be innovative and would help to make Marquette more of a tourist destination. There were no takers to this concept. In late October 2012 a new proposal developed calling for a botanical-ecological center to be placed at the top of the dock. It would be developed using community action and enthusiasm and many millions of dollars in grant money.

At the present time, the ore dock, though now standing alone, remains a dominant feature of Marquette's Lower Harbor. It is a symbol of the important role played by the iron ore industry in the central Upper Peninsula and, more specifically, Marquette.

Art and the Dock

Although time and the elements did not treat Ore Dock No. 6 well, the structure remained an important Marquette landmark. In 1967, it was the subject of a popular painting. Robert Thom of Birmingham, Michigan was commissioned by Michigan Bell Telephone to produce a painting of the structure unveiled in Marquette during *Michigan Week* (late May). This painting was part of a series dealing with Michigan history and is available through the Michigan Bureau of History in Lansing. Over the years, hundreds of amateur and professional photographers have taken photographs of the dock in various seasons of the year. In recent years, the dock has been used as a staging area for the 4th of July fireworks.

CHAPTER 3: APPROACH

The steel approach to the ore dock was 2,577 feet in length and wound its way from Fifth Street on the west to Lakeshore Blvd on the east through the heart of Marquette. In the process, train loads of iron ore were raised to eighty-five feet and seven inches to where they met the timber trestle east of Lakeshore.

With the commencement of construction on the dock proper, work immediately began on the approach. As early as March 1931, sections of the span were in Marquette awaiting construction. On April 8, C.E. Urbahns, general manager of DSS&A, announced that the railroad would have to relocate the main line through the west yards and remove other track in order to construct the new approach east of Fifth Street. The track work, along with the erection of the elevated approach between Fifth and Third Streets, was ready to proceed. Railroad crews realigned the track on land a half mile to the west. On May 25, work began on the foundation for the elevated approach at Fourth Street. Concrete crib walls were constructed westward from Fourth Street: 289 feet on the north side and 115 feet on the south side. Four days later, workmen began the excavation of the pier and abutment at the Fourth Street site. With this work completed from June 2- 12, concrete was poured for the Fourth Street pier and abutment. This work progressed slowly because little could be done until the end of the navigation season. Otherwise, the crew would be interfering with the old approach to Ore Dock No. 5, which was in use through the 1931 shipping season.

In late July, a major change was made to the type of material to be used in a portion of the approach. Originally, plans called for the approach between Fourth and Third Streets to be constructed of timber. It was found, however, that the price of steel had declined and a steel approach would add only $18,000 to the cost. Furthermore, the engineers with the DSS&A felt that the change would make the approach fireproof, aesthetically pleasing, and would demand low maintenance. As a result, the only portion constructed of timber was between South Lakeshore Blvd and the ore dock proper. The concrete foundations carrying the tracks over Fourth Street were completed by the end of July. Construction of the steel approach to Third Street was awarded to Wisconsin Bridge and Iron Company of Milwaukee, Wisconsin, while Merritt, Chapman & Whitney was to connect this portion of the approach to the wooden section. Fred Eastman was the man in charge of this part of the project. The first steel column to support the approach was erected midway between Third and Fourth Streets by September 19.

The approach was a steel trestle landing on concrete piers. The foundation piers were six feet deep and each one rested on eight piles. The trestle was supported by eleven sets of columns, or bents, of which four were the tower type, cross-laced to guard against side strain and torsion. The approach rose on a one percent grade between Fourth and Third Streets, and the increase from one street to the other was three feet. There was little difference in the length of the columns since the increase in height was accomplished by building the cement piers higher. The last of the piers were completed on October 3, and all that remained to be done was the steel work. The many steel braces, columns, girders, and other parts were fabricated in the Milwaukee plant of the company and were then shipped to Marquette for final riveting. In the plant, they were painted with one coat of red lead and oil, and in the field they received two coats of black graphite. It was planned to have fourteen carloads of steel to complete the job. The railroad ties, arriving from Oregon, were bolted to the trestle only when the job was completed.

By December 1931, attention concentrated on the new approach. At the end of that month, workmen were constructing the dock approach at the foot of Third Street. Some materials from the approach to Ore Dock No. 5 were used as needed on the new approach. The bents rose thirty-two feet above the ground on each side of the street. There was a twenty-four foot clearance between the two sides of each bent. Two steel girders, each measuring eighty feet in length by seven and-a-half feet in width and weighing thirty-one tons, were in the rail yards awaiting placement. The new rail approach, beginning at Fifth Street, was erected to a point a short distance from Third Street. The long runway was planned so that the grade for ore trains would be greatly diminished, as opposed to the old ore dock, whose approach began at Third Street. Concrete continued to be poured for the pedestals. It was planned to erect four steel towers and four steel bents between Fourth and Third Streets and one tower between Front Street and Lakeshore Blvd. The span over Front Street was forty-two feet above ground-level, about twenty-nine feet higher than the old span. The bents were even higher at Lakeshore near the dock, where the spans projected sixty-two feet above the ground at track level. Allowing for nine feet of steel, this left a clearance of fifty-three feet above Lakeshore Blvd. All other structural steel parts were placed on the approach between December 28, 1931 and March 1, 1932, with the final two coats of black graphite paint applied by April 20.

The approach was tested for the first time on June 1, when thirty cars were pushed up the structure. The new approach allowed three times the number of cars than the old approach. This, along with the enlarged capacity of the dock, allowed greater efficiency.

The tracks crossed Fifth Street at a grade consisting of dirt fill that was supported by concrete crib walls ending at a concrete abutment on the west side of Fourth Street. On the east side of Fourth Street, a concrete pier supported the steel span and the first span of the steel approach. From this point to the west side of Lakeshore Blvd, the train passed over a steel tower and bent type of construction. Concrete piers and footings supported the towers and bents.

The ore trains approached Fourth Street on a 1.22% grade which continued to a point approximately 145 feet east of the street. From this point to the west side of Front Street, the grade was 0.5855%. There, it changed to a 0.6603% grade and continued as such to the dock.

Alignment on the approach had two six degree curves. The first was 368 feet long to the right, and the second 380 feet long to the left. There was also one seven degree curve 252 feet to the right.

Over the years, the approach was maintained as needed. During the maintenance season of 1958, $21,320 was spent on improvements to the approach. The following year, another $29,124 was spent. During the winters of 1965-1966 and 1966-1967, construction work was carried out on the approach posts, bridge piling, and crib work. A complete inspection of the entire structure was conducted in July 1972, and the approach was found to be in fairly good condition. At the time, a cost repair estimate was made by the Soo Line. The repairs to the dock and its approaches would be $38,000.

The question of vandalism, trespass, liability, and fire has been raised and dealt with since the construction of the structure. The retaining wall at the base of the approach between Front and Third Streets provided a popular location for local youth to congregate in the late 1970s. In November 1977, one individual was injured in a fall. This was followed by complaints by adjacent property owners of harassment and the destruction of property. It was recommended that a fence be placed on the site and protruding bolts be removed from the wall. It seems, however, that the problem was solved without resorting to these measures.

In 1981, there was some renewed interest in rehabilitating the dock and its approach. A complete inspection of the dock showed that it would have to be rehabilitated if it were to be reopened. The report showed that most of the ties would have to be replaced. The approach needed many replacements, and it was recommended that the rails and switches be replaced with heavier gauge rails to more efficiently handle heavier loads. The Soo Line estimated proposed expenses for the dock and approach would be $625,000.

The status of the dock remained undecided. On March 8, 1985, Krech & Ojard Consulting Engineers, based in Duluth, Minnesota, released a report, "Removal Estimate of the Soo Line Ore Dock in Marquette MI," which had been ordered by the Michigan Department of Transportation. The demolition was to include the removal of the approach trestle to the dock. At the time, the cost estimate for the removal of the steel portion of the dock approach together with the timber decking and concrete piers was $70,635.

The approach and trestle dominated downtown Marquette until the winter of 2000, when it was dismantled. After debate over its historical value, the trestle over Front Street, along with its welcome sign, was also taken down. In 2005, the concrete abutments at Fourth Street were removed to make way for a bike path. A few years later, the last remnant of the approach and trestle, a single concrete abutment on the west side of Front Street, was demolished.

CHAPTER 4: TIMBER TRESTLE

The timber trestle was located in the city of Marquette between the end of the concrete portion of the ore dock and the timber pier on the east side of Lakeshore Blvd. It was 420 feet and consisted of 840,000 board feet per thousand. The incline on this portion of the approach varied from 685.09 feet on the west side to 687.17 feet at the top of the ore dock. It was, at first, planned to construct the entire approach with timber. After this portion of the approach had been constructed, however, the lower cost of steel during the Great Depression allowed steel to be used from Lakeshore Blvd westward.

Work on the timber trestle between the dock and Lakeshore Blvd commenced on May 29, 1931 with the placement of grillage supports for the substructure foundation. This work was completed in two months. As this work was completed, piles were driven and the approach bents placed between Lakeshore and the waterfront. By mid-June there were several hoists, pile drivers, and six barges in full operation. The first wooden approach trestles were also set into place. They were constructed in sections on the ground and then connected to one another by side timbers. The major timber work on the Lakeshore portion of the approach was completed by late August, and, by September 9, the ties for the rails were in place. Now all that could be done was to await the end of the navigation season when the old approach could be dismantled.

There are three added features on the trestle. One of the two stairways to the top of the dock was located on the south side of the structure. Nearby were the steps to the south walk onto the dock. A warming house, measuring 10' x 42', was located at the southeast corner of the trestle. Within the structure there were four rooms: the office (8'3" x 9'), the tool room (5'6" x 9'), the warming room (18'4" x 9'), and the toilet room (7'3" x9'). The water closet and urinal emptied directly into the lake waters below.

The timber trestle needed constant maintenance. The bridge piling and crib work was repaired during the winters of 1965-1966 and 1966-1967. Finally, the untreated dock timbers were replaced with rot resistant treated timbers.

The status of the dock remained undecided. On March 8, 1985, Krech & Ojard Consulting Engineers, based in Duluth, Minnesota, released a report, "Removal Estimate of the Soo Line Ore Dock in Marquette MI," which had been ordered by the Michigan Department of Transportation. The combined cost for the removal of the timber portion of the approach, the dock superstructure to elevation 610.35, and the outer timber tail trestle was estimated at $3,039,454.

Questions of vandalism, trespass, liability, and fire have been raised and dealt with since the construction of the structure. Originally, a three inch water pipe with three fire hose outlets, running the length of the structure, was fastened to the bent. The concern for fire prompted the DSS&A to employ a watchman. There were sabotage concerns during World War II, necessitating the employment of a twenty-four hour guard. Extra extinguishers were also added at the timber trestle area for added protection. In 1950, the possibility of using the dock to unload petroleum products and gasoline was discussed by the International Oil Company. The company wanted to run a pipeline along the dock to its storage tanks in the vicinity. DSS&A officials, citing a high fire danger to an extremely important facility, declined the offer even though it meant the loss of tanker car traffic on the line. The maze of timber on the trestle approach to the dock constantly caused concern for officials. In 1957, the first discussions were conducted concerning the replacement of the old timbers with fire retardant ones. This was done in a six year period during the 1960s. On August 20, 1961, two juvenile vandals brought the problem of fire to the attention of officials. Although the small fire only charred a bulletin board and was quickly extinguished, there was concern that more extensive damage could have been done. Although a fence already existed at the site, there was talk of placing a more secure barrier at the location.

As of March 2000, the timber trestle was gone from the scene. From it, crews salvaged nearly 100,000 board feet of timber. These timbers were easily sold to prospective buyers because of their fine condition and massive size.

Southwest aerial view of the dock and its approach, circa 1970.

Looking east from approach showing form for pedestals #6 to #11, June 21, 1931.

View looking east showing piles driven for approach bents. May 23, 1931.

West side of Fourth Street; concrete foundation of crib work. June 29, 1931.

Steel approach construction looking west from Third Street, October 9, 1931.

South elevation showing progress to date. October 11, 1931.

General view from the Dock No. 5 to the north showing progress of work to date, October 19, 1931.

Construction August 22, 1931.

Construction workers pour concrete, August 22, 1931.

View of south elevation showing the timber pattern during construction, August 22, 1931.

View looking east showing the south elevation, June 1990.

Close-up of chutes, June 1990.

Approach from Third Street looking west, June 1990.

View east on the south elevation from Lake Street, June 1990.

Area beneath the ore dock, June 1990.

Top of the ore dock looking west, June 1990.

Machinery for operating chutes, June 1990.

CHAPTER 5: ORE DOCK

The concrete dock, which for so long dominated Marquette's Lower Harbor, rests on thousands of pilings. It was connected to the shore by the approach trestle and a wooden walkway. Work on the site began on April 7, 1931, when the contractor from Merritt, Chapman & Whitney arrived and started arrangements for construction. Two days later, Gwin A. Whitney, president of Merritt, Chapman & Whitney, announced that construction had begun on the site of the ore dock itself. The first men were hired and began constructing the office while preparations were made to accept the pilings. Some 7,000 pilings were to be used for the foundation. Crews began to remove them from the dismantled Soo Line dock in Superior, Wisconsin, on April 8. These pilings ran fifty to seventy feet in length; there were more than enough of them at the Superior site for the new dock.

The first phase of construction was the installation of the foundation pilings. On April 12, J.G. Bazil, the engineer in charge, saw the arrival of a double load of untreated pilings and the pile driving hoist and associated equipment. The equipment was operational within twelve hours. The first load of pilings began to arrive from Superior on April 14. The first test piles were sunk on April 16-17, and, two days later, work began on the bearing pilings for the approach as the bents were placed in the water. This work was completed on April 22. At Superior, crews were working twenty-four hours a day to get the pilings out and shipped to Marquette. At the latter site, there was little space for a build-up of pilings. The bearing piles for the dock proper were sunk between April 22 and July 23. By April 27, two additional pile drivers had arrived so that one was used to drive batter piles and the other was used to assist with driving sheet piling. The additional equipment was needed because at the time, an average of 200 pilings were arriving each day and the drivers could barely keep up with them.

Office space became necessary as construction started. On April 9, Bazil began the renovation of a James Pickands Company building at the nearby coal dock for Merritt, Chapman & Whitney's officials and office staff. S.P. Berg, the engineer from the DSS&A, refitted the old commissary on South Lakeshore Blvd as office space for the inspectors, material clerks, timekeepers, and other clerical workers.

Meanwhile, a small fleet of work boats began to arrive at the site. On April 15, the tug *William A. Whitney* arrived from Superior with a scow in tow to be used to transport material from the shore as the dock extended into the water. Towards the end of the month, Merrill, Chapman & Whitney sent the scow *Four Spot* from Duluth carrying concrete forms and completely equipped with a mixing machine and other apparatus for mixing and pouring concrete.

At the dock site, work was progressing on schedule. By early May, a third of the pilings were in place, though progress had been slowed by the breakdown of a pile driver. On May 4, the laborers began to erect walling timber for the cribs and the bearing piles. Crews started to drive sheet piling for cribs on May 6. This type of piling was made by bolting three 4 x 12 timbers together with the center timber recessed several inches so as to form a groove into which a tongue, formed by a similar arrangement of timber, was slipped. Crib A was completed on May 18. One driver was used until the bearing pilings were completed, after which two drivers were put to use. This work was completed on July 23. Work on the batter piles commenced on May 14, and was completed by early June. Construction of movable forms for the substructure continued between May 18 and July 29. On May 26, men began framing the approach bents both in the water and on land. This work was completed on December 1. On the afternoon of July 7, the first of six concrete columns was poured at the site. Within two days, half of the column foundations were finished, with the schedule calling for the rest of them to be completed within the next few weeks. On July 22, approximately one-third of the concrete had been poured. All of the mixers and associated equipment were in excellent working order and work progressed rapidly. The first of the concrete cross beams, each weighing ten tons, connecting the dock's columns laterally, was swung into place on July 20.

The "water work," as the pile driving was called, was to be completed within a week. The last of the sheet piling was driven near the end of the dock, and this, along with cluster piling at several points along the dock, completed the work. A shipment of structured steel arrived but remained unused until the wooden trestle over Lakeshore Blvd was completed. Construction halted until the railroad tracks and the old approach were dismantled.

On June 8, once the pilings were in place, the dock's reinforced steel substructure was positioned. Once this was started, work began on the major concrete portion of the structure. The concrete equipment consisted of the scow, mixer, and a seventy foot concrete tower, or traveler, which would allow the concrete to be hoisted in a skip to the top of the dock. The traveler was erected on June 30 and dismantled on November 28. The old Spear Dock was renovated in order to construct and repair the precast tie beams. The first concrete work began on May 21; the beams were fabricated on shore and placed in the water as the first step in the foundation. This work at the dock continued until July 28. In the meantime, J.G. Olson, engineer in charge of construction, noted that sixty-five percent of the round pilings had been driven and the remainder of them were to arrive within ten days. Work was temporarily halted, however, when an air hose operating a saw which trimmed the tops of the pilings went out of operation. The crews driving the sheet piling were also slowed as they hit hard pan in the harbor bottom. As a result, concrete work was held up until the problem was solved.

The concrete work on the basic structure continued without incident. The concrete mattress was placed over the substructure dock between June 14 and July 30, and work on the concrete pedestals and fender continued from June 19 through August 4. The tie beams were set into place between July 20 and October 19. By mid-August, fifty-six piers of concrete columns, which formed the underside of the dock, were poured, leaving about half that number to be done before the foundation of the dock was complete. By August 20, all but nine sets of concrete columns were complete, with total completion planned within a week. While this work was underway, the superstructure form work, started on July 23, continued. It was completed on November 11.

At the east end of the dock was a large timber trestle structure. Constructed of treated and squared timbers, it was thirty feet in length, running the width of the dock. Attached to the concrete dock, this addition provided a stairway from the base of the dock to the top. Midway up the structure there is a landing which provided access to the walkway at the chute level. This structure, along with the stairs and walkway, was disassembled in 1999.

Work progressed on the pockets and chutes. During the last few months of 1931, some of the finishing work on the dock was completed. The outer end fender piles and approach fender piles were completed, the steel deck painted, the rails laid on the dock, and the deck plan placed on the dock proper.

The heart of the Ore Dock consists of seventy-five pockets on both sides of the structure. Each of the 150 pockets has a storage capacity of seven fifty ton cars of ore. The length of the facility, including the approach (which has since been removed) and the dock was 3,546 feet. The dock itself measures 969 feet from the beginning of concrete construction to the fender at the east end. The width of the top of the dock measures fifty-nine feet from side to side. The over-hanging deck which supports the hoists and motors measures 67' 9 ½" between the handrails.

Extending along the exterior face of the pockets on both sides of the dock and placed above the apron between the pocket doors and the hinge ends of the chutes was a plank walk. This walk provided access to the pocket openings. Four stairways anchored to the concrete face of the dock provided access to the walk. The stairways terminated at a landing approximately twelve feet above the walk, which was reached by a steel ladder. Steel railings provided adequate protection for workers using the stairs, landings, and walks.

The top of the dock was covered with a steel deck and four railroad tracks, with two tracks over each pocket. Eighteen inch steel beams running the length of the dock supported the rails. Four inch fir planking covered the deck except for the overhanging section.

Originally, night illumination on the top of the dock was provided by seventy-five 100-watt lamps suspended in strings of five between thirty foot high steel poles located sixty feet apart. Each of the lamps was equipped with a bowl reflector. The individual pockets were lighted on the interior by another 100-watt lamp located under the deck towards the front wall of the pockets. A 100-watt lamp on a goose neck bracket was located above the door openings on the exterior side. Throughout the structure there was adequate lighting on the fenders, stairways, and walks.

The fender, which ran the entire length of the dock, was six feet in above water and five feet in width from the outside face to the base of the columns. Two 14" x 14" oak wales, which extended two inches beyond the outside face of concrete, prevented vessels from making contact with the concrete fender. The circular outer end of the fender had two clusters of fifteen oak piles with exterior waling strips providing additional protection to boats.

Ships entered Marquette harbor from Lake Superior by way of channels dredged by the U.S. Army Corps of Engineers. Semaphores for day use (after 1944) and lights for night use signaled the captain whether to use the north or south slip.

The mooring posts on the fender are anchored to the concrete and were placed at intervals of thirty-six and forty-eight feet. A 2 ½ inch pipe hand rail, four feet above and on the inside of the fender, extended the entire length of the dock on both sides, providing protection for the seamen handling the lines and passing to and from the vessels. The chutes, aligned with the holds of the ship, were lowered, allowing the ore to slide into the waiting ship. As a result of this process, several ships could be loaded simultaneously, or, if there were no ships at the dock, the trains could continue to fill the pockets for the next arrival.

By 1932, the water approach to the dock had been dredged to a minimum depth of twenty-four feet below a mean low water elevation of 601.60 feet. The slips were eighty feet wide and extended from the shore some 650 feet. Beyond this point, a wider channel was dredged so that it was 125 feet wide at a distance of 850 feet from the bulkhead.

Major improvements were made at the end of the 1947 season. The wooden fenders on the dock were rebuilt and pile drivers re-drove the cluster piles. By mid-October, the pilings for the protective fenders at the outer end of the ore dock were re-driven. The cluster piles to the south, near Ripley's Rock, were also re-driven and tied with cable. On the south side of the dock, all of the pilings in the wood fender were re-driven but not cut off. The schedule called for work to be completed by the end of the month.

Due to the harsh weather conditions, repairs and improvements were constantly made on the dock. Early in 1953, it was observed that the overhead wiring on the upper deck had to be replaced. This work was completed by 1957. In 1961, poor lighting at the end of the dock necessitated the installation of a flood light and two lights twelve feet above the fender. The electric hoist motors went through gradual maintenance and repair at the rate of two motors per year between 1956 and the early 1960s. During the early 1960s, there were a number of seasons of heavy repairs made on the dock. During the winters of 1965-1966 and 1966-1967, general dock work was carried out along with the construction of approach posts, bridge pilings, and cribs. The wooden decking and walkways were also repaired at this time. Finally, the untreated dock timbers were replaced with rot-resistant treated timbers.

Due to lack of use, the approach, the wooden deck, and stairs of the dock deteriorated. This is best evidenced in a 1981 inspection produced by the railroad. Though the Soo Line maintained fences and warning signs, youths and adults alike, fascinated by the structure, continued to trespass. In the autumn of 1988, police discovered the skeleton of a local teenager, Timothy P. Alain, who had fallen to his death in the structure.

Due to lack of use and maintenance, by 1990, the dock had fallen into a state of disrepair. Wisconsin Central Ltd. was concerned that anyone walking on the dock ran the risk of being injured, as even the large timbers were weakened. Much of the stairway on the trestle at the east end of the dock was missing and could not be used. There was also concern that the steel parts of the dock and the bolts had been weakened by the ravages of time and neglect.

CHAPTER 6: CHUTES

The chutes and associated steel parts of the dock were the last major parts of the structure to be attached. McClintick & Marshall Corporation of Chicago furnished the steel for the chutes. As the concrete superstructure took shape between July 23 and November 11, 1931, work was started on the metal parts of the dock. On July 27, channels were riveted to the door frames and beginning on August 4, reinforced steel was placed on the superstructure. This work continued until November 11. Between August 22 and November 7, the concrete pockets were poured.

The steel doors and chutes were needed as work on the concrete dock progressed. On July 7, a shipment of 500 tons of steel, consisting largely of pocket doors, arrived from Duluth. In total, approximately 3,000 tons of steel would be used on the dock.

There would be seventy-five pockets on each side of the dock for a total of 150 pockets. By the middle of August, construction of the pockets was underway. Outside forms, together with the steel doors, were put in place on six pockets on August 12. Inside forms for an additional twenty pockets were then placed. This part of the job was time consuming and the work did not progress as rapidly as anticipated. The reason for the slow work was the fact that the forms had to be built separately before being put into place. They were heavy clumsy wooden affairs that required much maneuvering with derricks before they were in the correct position. Because the steel work was being constructed in other parts of the country, absolute accuracy in this work was essential, so that the concrete portions of the pockets and the upper dock structure would fit correctly on the steel work. By September 9, ten sets of pockets had been completed and the concrete forms were removed and placed in position for additional pockets. By the middle of September, nearly twenty-five percent of the pockets had been completed.

Work was ahead of schedule on the concrete pockets, the last of which was completed by mid-November, prior to the start of the winter season. After completion of the concrete pockets, concentration shifted to the structural steel work on the dock. Once the chutes were painted and installed, work began on the dock proper. The deck steel was set into place between October 9, 1931, and January 20, 1932, and during the same period of time the outer end trestle was finished. The 150 hoists were completed by November 16, and they were installed between December 18 1931, and May 10, 1932. By December 11, ninety percent of the structural steel was in place and about thirty-five percent of the 150 chutes were installed. Jernsted Electrical Company completed their work between October 2, 1931 and April 29, 1932.

The heart of the Ore Dock consists of 75 pockets on both sides of the structure. Each of the 150 pockets had a storage capacity of seven fifty ton cars of ore. The ore was dropped directly into the pockets and the train left the dock. From a mean low water elevation of 601.60 feet, the elevation of the dock is eighty-five feet seven inches. Further, it is forty-three feet three inches from water level to the hinge pin of the chutes. Each of the pockets has a floor angle of forty-seven and one half degrees, one side of which is flush with the east wall, leaving a fillet corner only on the west wall. Each chute weighs four and one half tons and measures thirty- six feet in length and ranges in width from seven feet two and one half inches at the hinge or butt end down to four feet ten inches inside at the spout end. Electrically powered hoists raised and lowered each of the chutes individually. A 3/8 inch by 5 ½ inch steel cable connects the hoist to the chute. Each set of eleven hoists was operated by one motor. The only difference occurs in the outer section of the dock where one motor operated a set of nine hoists. The motors were twenty-five HP, three phase, 440 volt, sixty cycle type.

The width of the top of the dock measures fifty-nine feet from side to side. The overhanging deck which supports the hoists and motors measures sixty-seven feet nine and one half inches between the handrails. The steal pocket doors, located at an angle approximately twenty degrees to the face of the pockets, were controlled by double sliding arms. These doors were raised and lowered by the chute hoists. Both the chutes and doors could be raised or lowered while ore was running from the pockets. The door frames are imbedded in the concrete and are provided with an extension projecting four feet beyond the front wall face of the concrete. This was built up of a bottom steel apron on the same slope as pocket floors and with side cheek plates to which the chutes are attached. Nothing extended beyond the fender line. The clearance point, or the vertical projection of the fender line to the inner section of the bottom of the chute when raised in an upright position, was at a height of forty-five feet six inches above the mean low water level of 601.60 feet.

Extending along the exterior face of the pockets on both sides of the dock was a plank walk which is placed above the apron between the pocket doors and the hinge ends of the chutes. This walk provided access to the pocket openings. Four stairways anchored to the concrete face of the dock provided access to the walk. The stairways terminate at a landing approximately twelve feet above the walk, which is reached by a steel ladder from this point. Steel railings provided adequate protection for workers using the stairs, landings, and walks.

The electric hoist motors went through gradual maintenance and repair at the rate of two motors per year between 1956 and the early 1960s. In the later 1960s costly steel work on the chute liners and ore pocket doors and linings was also completed.

Use of the Ore Dock ended in 1971. A complete inspection conducted in July 1972 found the dock and its approach to be in fairly good condition. The major work required on the dock had to be the straightening of chute angles, the installation of splash shields at the chutes, and some welding on the chutes. A later inspection showed that all of the electric motors which were last operated in the spring of 1973 appeared to be in good condition.

A cost repair estimate was made by the Soo Line in 1974. The repairs to the dock and its approaches would be $38,000 and the installation of splash shields would require an additional $6,000. Although, at the time, there was talk of shipping 1.5 million tons through the ore dock, nothing further developed beyond the initial discussions and cost estimates.

In 1981 there was some renewed interest in rehabilitating the dock and its approaches. A complete inspection of the dock showed the repairs that were required to reopen. The report showed that the shakers and doors were beyond repair and would have to be replaced and 93 front covers and 81 rear covers on the chutes were missing. The hoists would have to be repaired along with the stairs. The Soo Line estimated that the dock electrical equipment and the motors would cost $19,000.

Due to the lack of use the approach, the wooden deck and stairs of the dock deteriorated. This is best evidenced in a 1981 inspection produced by the railroad. The Soo Line maintained fences and warning signs but both youths and adults, fascinated by the structure, trespassed. In the autumn of 1988, two local teenagers walking on the structure discovered a skeleton. A transient, 17 year old, Timothy P. Alain had climbed to the top of the dock some time in the past and had fallen to his death in a chute, which he was unable to climb out of. In 1990 the chutes and other metal attachments to the dock remained in place but were slowly falling victim to time and the elements. By 2000, most of the steel attachments to the dock had been removed, the chutes, however, remain.

As of 2013 Ore Dock NO. 6 the property of the city of Marquette, stands as a massive sentinel, dominating Marquette's Lower Harbor. The Marquette City Commissioner authorized a structural study of the dock conducted during 2013-2014. At this time there are no definite plans for the dock by the city. It remains a Marquette icon enjoyed by residents and visitors alike.

Bibliography

Aerial Survey, Marquette, Michigan. Lansing, Michigan: Abrams Aerial Survey Company, 1931.

"Amos R. Harlow Bought First Land in City," *Mining Journal*, 7/8/1935.

Armstrong, William F., Sr. "Description of Loading Docks Built to Handle Iron Ore from Marquette, Michigan, 1855-1929," manuscript, John M. Longyear Research Library, Regional History Center: Marquette, Michigan (hereafter cited: JML/MRHC).

Armstrong, William F., Sr. "Statement of Corporations . . . Connected with the DSS&A Ry. Co.," 1929, manuscript, JML/MRHC.

---. "Duluth, South Shore & Atlantic Railway Co. Ore Dock No. 6, 1931," *Harlow's Wooden Man* 19/2 (Spring 1983), 9-11.

---. "Duluth, South Shore & Atlantic Railway Co. Ore Dock No. 6, 1931," *Harlow's Wooden Man* 19:2 (Spring 1983), 9-11.

---. "Duluth, South Shore & Atlantic Railway Co. Ore Dock No. 6, 1931," *The Soo*, 7:2 (April 1985), 34-35.

---. "Historical Sketch of the Marquette Iron Range," January 1932, manuscript, JML/MRHC

---. "Railroad History of Marquette," *Mining Journal*, 1/22, 1/23, 1/25, 1932.

---. "Shipments of Iron Ore from Mines on Marquette Range via Docks for Shipment via Lake, 1846-1929," manuscript, JML/MRHC.

--- to H.F. Schmidt, Marquette, Michigan, 3/7/1944, in Chief Engineer's File, DA-c-1-74, Wisconsin Central Ltd., manuscript, Northern Michigan University Archives: Marquette, Michigan (hereafter cited: NMUA).

Anonymous. "Duluth, South Shore and Atlantic Railway," (Contract 1151), 12/7/1936, Wisconsin Central Ltd., manuscript, NMUA.

"Articles of Association of the South Shore Dock Company," March 11, 1931 in Miscellaneous Records #1116, Vault, Clerk's Office, Court House, Marquette, Michigan.

Barry, Richard J. "History of the Duluth, South Shore and Atlantic Railway and Its Predecessors," no date, manuscript, JML/MRHC.

Beard's Directory of Marquette County, Michigan. Detroit: Hadger& Bryce, 1873;

Berg, S.P. to T.Z. Krumm, Marquette, Michigan, 10/14/1947, in Chief Engineer's File, 1920-1980, DA-c-1-74 (vol. 1), Wisconsin Central Ltd., manuscript, NMUA.

"Begin Tearing Down Trestle Over Front Street," *Mining Journal*, 12/11/1931.

"Begin Today on New Ore Dock Work - Piling Shipped," *Mining Journal*, 4/9/1931.

Berg, S.P. to T.Z. Krumm, Marquette, MI, 10/14/1947, in Chief Engineer's File, DA-c-1-74 (v. 1), Wisconsin Central Ltd., manuscript, NMUA.

Bervelheimer, Chuck, et. al. “Developmental Criteria for the Lower Harbor, Marquette, Michigan,” 1981, manuscript, JML/MRHC.

Birds Eye View of Marquette Michigan, 1871, Marquette County Historical Society, Marquette, Michigan.

Brubaker, N.A. to R.G. Gehrz, “Property Damage Complaints concerning Ore Dock at Marquette, Michigan,” Gladstone, Michigan, 3/2/1978, in Chief Engineer's File, 1920-1981, DA-c-1-74 (v. 1), Wisconsin Central, Ltd., manuscript, NMUA.

“Business Men Pledged Aid to Railway Lines,” *Mining Journal*, 4/10/1931.

“Certificate of Dissolution,” August 27, 1943, filed September 13, 1943 in Miscellaneous Records #1116, Vault, Clerk's Office, Court House, Marquette, Michigan.

Chase, Lew Allen. “History of Marquette, Marquette County and the Lake Superior Region,” *Mining Journal*, 10/10/1931.

“Chicago Firm Will Furnish Steel for Dock,” *Mining Journal*, 4/3/1931.

Clayton, W. “Early Settlement of Marquette, Michigan,” *Magazine of Western History*. 8:3 (July 1888), 271-280.

"Concrete Ore Dock," Chief Engineer's File, 1920-1981, DAc-1-74 (v. 1), Wisconsin Central Limited, manuscript, NMUA.

"Concrete Work is Delayed on New Ore Dock," *Mining Journal,* 5/29/1931.

"Concrete Work on Dock Ahead of Schedule," *Mining Journal*, 10/19/1931.

"Concrete Work on Dock to be Finished Soon," *Mining Journal*, 7/22/1931.

"Construction on Dock Job Started," *Mining Journal*, 4/14/1931.

"Construction Progress Statements between April 7, 1931 and May 10, 1932," Wisconsin Central Ltd., manuscript, NMUA.

"Construction Progress Statement, Marquette Ore Dock," Wisconsin Central Ltd., manuscript, NMUA.

"Contract between DSS&A and Merritt, Chapman and Whitney," April 1, 1931, Wisconsin Central Ltd., manuscript, NMUA.

"Details of Warming House," No. 1918, DSS&A, Engineering Department, 1931, Wisconsin Central Ltd., manuscript, NMUA.

"Dock Approach Being Erected at Rapid Rate," *Mining Journal*, 10/3/1931.

"Dock Approach Plans Changed by South Shore," *Mining Journal*, 7/28/1931.

"Dock Builders Preparing for Concrete Work, *Mining Journal*, 4/28/1931.

"Dock Hand Dies of Injuries in Lake Plunge," *Mining Journal*, 12/18/1931.

"Dock Worker Is Badly Injured in 45 Foot Fall," *Mining Journal*, 12/15/1931.

"Dock Worker Is Painfully Hurt," *Mining Journal*, 10/2/1931.

"Dock Workers Contribute to Needy Families," *Mining Journal*, 1/26/1932.

"Dredges Begin Work Here on Harbor Bottom," *Mining Journal*, 6/14/1931.

"DSS&A Authority for Expenditure," 2/27/1953, Chief Engineer's File, DA-c-1-74-14, Wisconsin Central Ltd., manuscript, NMUA.

Dunbar, Willis F. *All Aboard! A History of Railroads in Michigan.* Grand Rapids, Michigan: Eerdmans Publishing Co., 1969.

---. *Michigan: A History of the Wolverine State*. Grand Rapids, Michigan: Eerdmans Publishing Co., 1980.

Dunham, Della and Margaret W. Read. "History of Marquette Harbor," *Mining Journal*, 6/13/1917.

Durocher, Aurele A. "Duluth, South Shore and Atlantic Railroad Company," *The Railway and Locomotive Historical Society Bulletin*, No. 111 (1964), 7-81.

Elliott, Frank W. *When Railroad Was King: The Nineteenth Century Railroad Era in Michigan*. Lansing, Michigan: Michigan Historical Commission, 1965."

"$80,000 Harbor Job Is OKed for Marquette," *Mining Journal*, 4/25/1932.

Engels, B.E. Milwaukee, Wisconsin, 7/20/1943, in Marquette Concrete Ore Dock. Electric Power, Wiring and Fixtures, Chief Engineer's File, DA-c-1-74, WisconsinCentral Ltd., manuscript, NMUA.

"Estimated Removal Cost, Marquette Ore Dock," 4/19/1977, in Concrete Ore Dock, Chief Engineer's File, 1920-May 1981, DA-c-1-74 (vol. 1), Wisconsin Central Ltd., manuscript, NMUA.

"Fast Progress Being Made on Dock Approach," *Mining Journal*, 12/30/1931.

"First Boat Is Loaded at New Ore Dock Here," *Mining Journal*, 6/7/1932.

"First Lake Shipments of Iron Ore . . . 1855," *Mining Journal*, 10/1/1938.

"Ford Ore Boat to Take Cargo Here June 5th," *Mining Journal*, 5/21/1932.

"Forms Set for Six Pockets on New Dock Here," *Mining Journal*, 8/13/1931.

"4th St. Concrete Abutments Demolished to Make Way for New Bike Path," *Mining Journal*, 9/13/2005.

Gehrz,R.G. to D.M. Cavanaugh and L.L. Wasnick, Minneapolis, Minnesota, 3/6/1978, in Chief Engineer's File, 1920-1981, DA-c-1-74 (v. 1), Wisconsin Central, Ltd., manuscript, NMUA.

Gove Associates, Inc. *City of Marquette Lower Harbor Redevelopment Plan, Marquette, Michigan*. Kalamazoo, Michigan: Gove Associates, Inc., 1986.

"Harbor Master's Report," in Marquette Police Departmtent Annual Report - 1971, on file at City Hall, Police Department, Marquette, Michigan.

Hart, D.L. to A.S. Krefting, Stevens Point, WI, 10/10/1961, in Chief Engineer's File, DA-c-1-74-14, Wisconsin Central Ltd., manuscript, NMUA.

Hart, D.L. to T.R. Klingel, Minneapolis, Minnesota, 1/8/1974, in Chief Engineer's File, 1920-1981, DA-c-1-74 (vol. 1), Wisconsin Central Ltd., manuscript, NMUA.

"History of Marquette Harbor," cited in "Transportation Plan," City of Marquette, Draft: September 16, 1986, 47-51, in Clerk's Office, City Hall, Marquette, Michigan.

"Huge Concrete Column Being Built for Dock," *Mining Journal*, 7/9/1931.

Hyde, Charles K. *The Upper Peninsula of Michigan: An Inventory of Historic Engineering and Industrial Sites*. Washington, D.C.: Government Printing Office, 1978.

"Investigation of Skeleton Brought to Close by Police," *Mining Journal*, 11/8/1988.

"Jones & Laughlin Expanded Operations at Tracy Mine During Past Decade," *Mining Journal*, 5/29/1970.

"Kelley's Suit Seeks Removal of 6 Marquette Ore Docks," *Mining Journal*, 11/20/1986.

Kitzman, Betty Lou. "First Pocket Ore Dock Built in Marquette 100 Years Ago," *Mining Journal*, 9/6/1957.

"Lake Shore to Install Dock Hoists," *Mining Journal*, 11/20/1931.

Lake Superior Mining and Manufacturing News, [newspaper] 6/18/1868.

Lancour, Jenny. "Skeleton Found in Ore Chute," *Mining Journal*, 10/20/1988.

"Last Carload of Ore Shipped from Tracy Mine in Negaunee," *Mining Journal*, 7/24/1971.

"Lease between DSS&A and the Marquette, Houghton and Ontonagon Railroad," 1931, manuscript, Wisconsin Central Ltd., NMUA.

Liber 63, 8; Liber 108, 44; Liber 109, 119, 121; Liber 362, 600-609, in Register of Deeds, Court House, Marquette, Michigan.

Lithograph of the city of Marquette, Michigan 1881, filed at the JML/MRHC.

Lowe, Kenneth S. "Harbor Hearing," *Mining Journal*, 2/26/1957.

"Lower Harbor Ore Dock Painting to Be Unveiled Here," *Mining Journal*, 5/20/1967.

Magnaghi, Russell M. *Bibliographic Survey and Scope of Work for Historical Documentation of the Marquette Ore Dock and Its Appraoches, Marquette, Michigan (ICC-89-M-1562-Q)*.Washington, D.C.: Interstate Commerce Commission, 1989.

"Make Progress on South Shore Dock," *Mining Journal*, 8/20/1931.

"Many Docks Were Constructed Here in Past Hundred Years," *Mining Journal*, 7/14/1956.

"Many Pockets Completed on New Dock Here," *Mining Journal*, 9/9/1931.

Marquette City Directory, 1929. Detroit: R.L. Polk & Company, 1929, 266.

Marquette-Ishpeming-Negaunee, Michigan City Directory. Kansas City, MO: R.L. Polk & Company, 1989, 91.

"Marquette Labor Employed on Dock," *Mining Journal*, 5/14/1931.

Marquette Lower Harbor Ore Dock Report. Marquette, Michigan: Marquette Area Chamber of Commerce Tourist Council, Ore Dock Committee, 1986.

Marquette, Michigan, 1888. (New York: Sanborn & Company, 1888) all maps deposited at the JML/MRHC, pp. 2-3.

Marquette, Michigan, 1892. (New York: Sanborn Company, 1892), p. 3.

Marquette, Michigan, 1897. (New York: Sanborn Company, 1897), pp. 2-3.

Marquette, Michigan, 1904. (New York: Sanborn Company, 1904), p. 3.

Marquette, Michigan, 1911. (New York: Sanborn Company, 1911), pp. 16, 18.

Marquette, Michigan, 1917. (New York: Sanborn Company, 1917), pp. 10, 12, 15.

Marquette, Michigan, 1928. (New York: Sanborn Company, 1928), pp. 6, 10.

Marquette, Michigan, 1928 with 1934 and 1946 Additions. (New York: Sanborn Map Company, 1946), pp. 4, 6.

"Marquette Ore Dock," 6/19/1932, Wisconsin Central Ltd., manuscript, NMUA.

"Marquette's Iron Ore Docks," December 1966, manuscript, JML/MRHC.

Marquette *Mining Journal*, 1931-2012. Copies are available for onsite use with copying possible at: Marquette Regional History Center, Northern Michigan University Archives; Peter White Public Library, Marquette, Michigan.

Mining Journal 4-29-1924, 7-11-1930, 1-2-1932, 7-7-1959, 5-20-1967, 9-3-1976, 5-30-1986, 11-20-1986, 5-7-1989, 6-10-1998, 12-10-1999, 12-17-1999, 1-12-2000, 3-24-2000, 2-22-2005, 1-27-2006, 9-23-2006, 9-26-2006, 6-27-2007, 10-30-2012

Monroe, M.J. "Ore Yard Tracks at Marquette," 4/29/1981, in Chief Engineer's File, 1920-1981, DA-c-1-74 (vol. 1), Wisconsin Central Ltd., manuscript, NMUA.

"New Dock Will Be Completed in Short Time," *Mining Journal*, 2/10/1932.

"New Ore Dock Built Entirely of Reinforced Concrete," *Railway Age* 94:9 (March 4, 1933), 326-328.

"New Ore Dock Rapidly Nearing Completion," *Mining Journal*, 11/3/1931.

"New Ore Dock Ready to Load Cargo June 5th," *Mining Journal*, 6/3/1932.

Nilsen, G.A. "Inspection of Marquette's Ore Dock," 4/10/1981, in Chief Engineer's File, 1920-1981, DAc-1-74 (vol. 1), Wisconsin Central Ltd., manuscript, NMUA.

Nilsen, G.A. and A.S. Krefting. Marquette, MI, 10/3/1961, in Chief Engineer's File, 1920-1981, DA-c-1-74 (v. 1), Wisconsin Central Ltd., manuscript, NMUA.

Northern Michigan University Archives, Marquette, Michigan. Manuscript materials, dock and approach plans, and blueprints have been deposited here.

Nute, Grace L. *Lake Superior*. Indianaoplis, Indiana: The Bobbs-Merrill Company, 1944.

"Ore Unsalable, Prittenen Says of Mine Closing," *Mining Journal*, 2/5/1971.

Pearson, B.E. to A.S. Krefting. Minneapolis, 8/21/1957; DSS&A Authority for Expenditure, 3/16/1959, in Chief Engineer's File, 1920-1981, DA-c-1-74 (v. 1), Wisconsin Central Ltd., manuscript, NMUA.

Pearson, B.E. to Harold J. Ness, "Proposed 1 ½ Million Ton Ore Movement - Marquette," Minneapolis, Minnesota, 1/4/1974, in Chief Engineer's File, 1920-1981, DA-c-1-74 (vol. 1), Wisconsin Central Ltd., manuscript, NMUA.

Peterson, W.B. to D.M. Cavanaugh, "Marquette Ore Dock," Minneapolis, Minnesota, 5/11/1981, in Chief Engineer's File, 1920-1981, DA-c-1-74 (vol. 1), Wisconsin Central Ltd., manuscript, NMUA.

Plaindealer [newspaper], 6/15/1868.

"Prepare to Drive Piling for Dock," *Mining Journal*, 4/16/1931.

"Purchase Agreement between the DSS&A and the South Shore Dock Company," 11/9/1931, Wisconsin Central Ltd., manuscript, NMUA.

"Rail Repair Crew Near Finish of Jobs on Ore Dock Here," *Mining Journal*, 4/15/1967.

Rankin, Ernest H. "The Founding of the Port of Marquette," *Inland Seas*. 32:1 (Spring 1976), 3-16.

"Razing of Old Ore Dock Has Been Started," *Mining Journal*, 12/2/1931.

"Rehabilitate Main Track from Marquette to Hogan's Ore Yard, 9.0 Miles," 5/11/1981, in Chief Engineer's File, 1920-1981, DA-c-1-74 (vol. 1), Wisconsin Central Ltd., manuscript, NMUA.

"Removal Estimate of the Soo Line Ore Dock in Marquette, MI," Duluth, Minnesota: Krech & Ojard Consulting Engineers, 1985, 1, in Marquette Conc. Ore Dock, Chief Engineer's File, DA-c-1-74 (v. 2), May 1981, Wisconsin Central Ltd., manuscript, NMUA.

"Repairs Eyed at Docks: Workers Here Furloughed," *Mining Journal*, 12/18/1965.

Report of A.H. Young, Gladstone, Michigan, 8/29/1961, in Chief Engineer's File, 1920-1981, DA-c-1-74 (v. 1), Wisconsin Central Ltd., manuscript, NMUA.

"Report of the Harbor Master" in "Marquette Police Department Annual Report," 1967-1971, filed in Police Department, City Hall, Marquette, Michigan.

"Report on the Valuation of the DSS&A Railway as of June 30, 1911," manuscript, JML/MRHC.

R.L. Polk & Company's 1910 Marquette City and County Directory. Detroit: R.L. Polk & Company, 1910.

Sargent, Bud. "Police Await Dental Records in Skeleton Probe," *Mining Journal*, 10/22/1988.

---. "Trestle Debate: Meetings Set on City 'Entrance' Section," *Mining Journal*, 12/14/1999.

---. "Huge Amounts of Wood Coming out of Rail Trestle," *Mining Journal*, 12/19/1999

---. "Ore Dock Rail Trestle Coming Down," *Mining Journal*, 12/29/1999.

Sawyer, Alvah L. *A History of the Northern Peninsula of Michigan*, 3 vols. Chicago, Illinois: The Lewis Publishing Company, 1911.

Schneider, Dave. "Landmark May Come Down," *Mining Journal*, 4/19/1990.

Simi, J.A. to A.S. Krefting, Marquette, MI, 12/4/1964, in Chief Engineer's File, DA-c-1-74-14, Wisconsin Central Ltd., manuscript, NMUA.

"Skeleton Found in Ore Dock Identified," *Mining Journal*, 10/25/1988.

"Skeleton Probe Hits Record Snag," *Mining Journal*, 10/24/1988.

Solether, P.L. to H.F. Schmidt, 5/10/1950, in Chief Engineer's File, 1920-1981, DA-c-1-74 (v. 1), Wisconsin Central Ltd., manuscript, NMUA.

South Shore Dock Company to First National Bank, Minneapolis, Minneapolis, 6/26/1932, Wisconsin Central Ltd., manuscript, NMUA.

"South Shore Dock Company," *Poor's Railroad Volume, 1937.* New York: Poor's Publishing Company, 1937, pp. 2013, 2021-2022.

"South Shore Probably Will Begin Building of New Dock this Year," *Mining Journal*, 3/30/1929.

"South Shore Reorganization to Be Completed this Year," *Mining Journal*, 5/10/1949.

"Steel Column for Approach to Dock Built," *Mining Journal*, 9/19/1931.

Swanson, Scott. "Marquette Trestle will be Removed," *Mining Journal*, 1/29/2006.

"Tax Rolls," 1941-present, in Treasurer's Office, Marquette County Court House, Marquette, Michigan.

Third of Piling for Railroad's Dock is Driven," *Mining Journal*, 5/8/1931.

"Tilden Mine Ore Movement: Summary of Estimate (Railroad Prices) [1974]," in Chief Engineer File, 1920- 1981, DA-c-1-74 (v. 1), Wisconsin Central Ltd., manuscript, NMUA.

"Tourist Council Examining Uses for Ore Dock," *Mining Journal*, 5/30/1986.

"Trestle Removal, Dock Sale Opposed," *Mining Journal*, 4/5/1989.

"Two Contracts for Dock Work Awarded Here," *Mining Journal*, 4/8/1931.

"Two Pile Drivers Brought Here for Dock Work," *Mining Journal*, 4/25/1931.

www.ingramcontent.com/pod-product-compliance
Ingram Content Group UK Ltd.
Pitfield, Milton Keynes, MK11 3LW, UK
UKHW041923190726
13854UKWH00003B/1416